Memory
Games

MEMORY GAMES

EASY WAYS TO KEEP YOUR MIND SHARP

JACK BOTERMANS
AND HELEEN TICHLER

Sterling Publishing Co., Inc.
New York

MEMORY GAMES

There comes a time in life when you discover your memory isn't quite as "fit" as it used to be. "Now what was I going to do?" is a question you ask yourself much too often. You regularly misplace objects that you just had in your hand a minute ago. Or you were just about to make an important point but suddenly don't remember what it was you were going to say. If you're lucky, these minor mishaps aren't as prevalent until after you've turned forty. But whenever it begins, once it begins, panic quickly sets in. Is it only just the beginning of the end? "I really hope it doesn't go on like this," you cry. And we're here to tell you that it doesn't have to.

There is hope!

A great deal of research has been conducted and published on the workings of the brain and how it is affected by the aging process. But we're not going to elaborate here on how your memory works. Instead, this book offers you a number of exercises, tests, and tips combined with interesting and revealing bits of information to help train your memory every day. "Remembering" requires that you activate pieces of information that have been stored in your memory

— and that's where the problems usually begin. "It's on the tip of my tongue," and that accompanying niggling feeling, is probably not unknown to you.

"Use your brain!" is the battle cry of this publication. The brain deteriorates when it's not used actively, but there's a lot you can do to keep your memory functioning optimally. In addition to solving puzzles and completing exercises, it's also important to remain involved with things happening around you. The games, puzzles, exercises, and tests in this book offer a pleasant, relaxing way to keep you mentally stimulated.

Memory Games is a book for everyone, whether you have a sharp memory or one that could use a bit of honing. Open it to any given page and begin with any exercise that attracts or interests you. After a while you will encounter new subjects that you are unfamiliar with. And eventually you'll discover that you're having increasingly more fun boosting your brain power and giving your memory a good pick-me-up!

STRUCTURE OF THE BOOK

Every exercise belongs to a particular category. Each category has to do with the functioning of particular brain properties. For the list of categories, see the next page.

Practice makes perfect. If you practice regularly, you'll have less and less need to tie a knot in your handkerchief or to write on the palm of your hand to remember errands or appointments.

ASIAN CONFUSION

The letters of this word are all mixed up. Try to put the seven letters in the right order and discover the correct word.

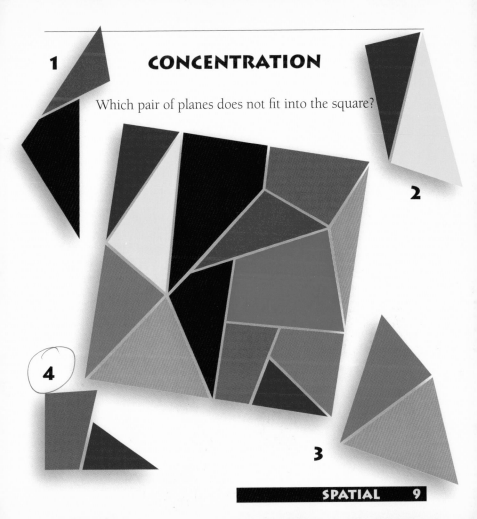

CONCENTRATION

Which pair of planes does not fit into the square?

A GAME OF CARDS

There's something strange about these cards. What is it?

CONCENTRATION

WOMEN GOVERN THE WORLD

And this illustration is the ultimate proof of it.

EIGHT ROSES

Look closely at these roses for about a minute, so you can remember them well. Now turn the next page and follow the instructions for the second part of this test on page 15.

TIP

Crossword puzzles are a pleasant activity and keep your vocabulary in good shape. They also promote mental flexibility and after a while you'll need less and less time to find the word you want. Select the level of puzzle that suits you, and try to solve the puzzle as quickly as possible. Don't dwell too long on a particular word, but do continue and don't forget to take a breather of a minute or so once in a while so that your concentration remains optimal.

DID YOU KNOW THAT...

... immediately after birth, there is a marked difference between girls and boys in how they react and behave? Girls are quicker to respond to facial expressions and spoken words. Girls also usually start to talk — and make whole sentences — at an earlier age than boys. Boys, on the other hand, stand up, walk, and run at an earlier age than girls. Their spatial intelligence is also developed at an earlier age than that of girls.

EIGHT ROSES

Without looking at page 12,
draw a circle to indicate the ninth rose.

DO YOU HAPPEN TO KNOW WHAT TIME...

Knowing that one of the clocks is seven hours ahead and the other seven hours behind, can you tell which of the clocks indicates the right time?

And which clock indicates the right time if you know that one clock is five hours ahead and one five hours behind?

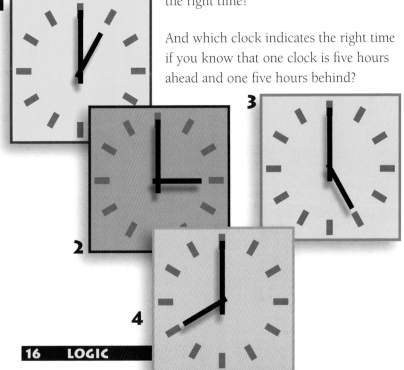

ARITHMETIC

Which number should replace the question mark?

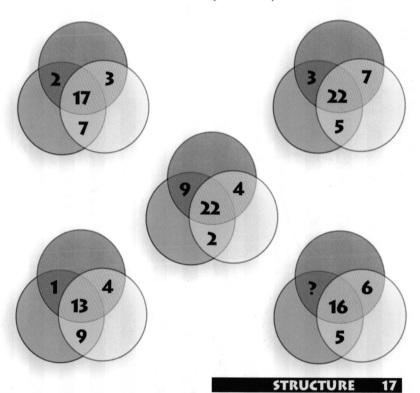

THE RIGHT SEQUENCE?

Which square does not belong in this series?

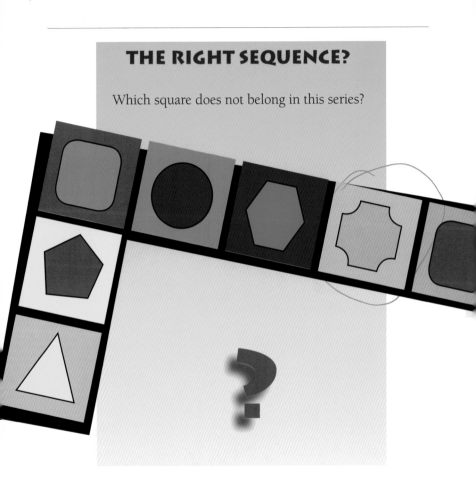

BERRY PUZZLE

How many berries should be on the leaves at the bottom?

THE EYES OF A CARPENTER

How many boards are visible?

ALPHABET PUZZLE

Add the letter Z to this plan, but in such a way that all the letters of the alphabet are represented only once.

SEEK AND YE SHALL FIND

Look closely at the four ice-cream vendors and find the one who's different from the others.

HOW'S YOUR WORLD HISTORY?

Answer the following questions:

1. Who was the first person to set foot on the moon on July 21, 1969?

2. Who introduced the miniskirt in the 1950s?

3. Who said in 1908, "I'm going to produce a car for the masses"?

4. Who was the first person to reach the South Pole, in 1911?

A QUESTION OF COINS

Lay out 10 coins on a table, in two rows as shown below. Move 3 coins from one row and one coin from the other so that 5 rows of 4 coins are created. You should not touch any of the other coins and you're not allowed to stack any coins.

HIDDEN NUMBER

Which number belongs in the square with the question mark?

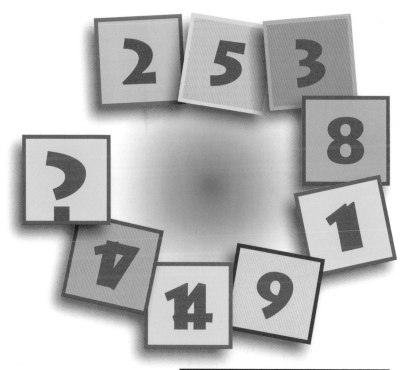

WOODEN MYSTERY

Examine this clog closely for about a minute. Try to memorize what it looks like. Then turn to page 29 for the rest of this test.

TIP

The memory is a little like a muscle: the more you use it, the more supple it will be. One of the methods to remember a number of things is to link them. For example, you need to borrow a book at the library, to buy a new pencil, and to get a pound of coffee. To help you remember this, you imagine you're going to write a book with a brown pencil.

DID YOU KNOW THAT...

...in school, Einstein wasn't all that good at arithmetic? Reading, writing, spelling, and arithmetic were not his strong points. He couldn't talk until he was three years old. Most of his life his thoughts were without words. His accomplishments mostly had to do with the visualizing of ideas in the area of time and space relations.

WOODEN MYSTERY

Can you tell what the difference is between the clog
on page 26 and this one?

AN INSEPARABLE DUO

Take two pieces of string, each about 3 feet (1m) long. Tie these around your wrists and those of a friend or family member (not too tight) as shown in the photo below. Now try to disengage yourselves from each other, without untying the knots or cutting the string.

FAMOUS MOVIE STARS

Five famous movie stars and they're all a bit messed up. That is to say, the letters of their names are. Can you order these letters in such a way that we know what their names are?

AGERT ORABG

EMA SEWT

TAZEHBILE RATYOL

IRDOS YDA

AGREC ELKYL

THE GREENGROCER

Giuseppe Arcimboldo (a sixteenth-century Italian painter) was a pioneer in the field of metamorphoses. Look closely at this portrait, and try to find as many kinds of vegetables and fruit as you can.

THE FLOATING DOT

Is this dot floating exactly in the middle of the inside triangle?

LOOK FOR THE WOMAN OF THE HOUSE

Can you find the wife?

BRAINTEASER

Which letter should replace
the question mark?

GAME OF MARBLES

Which figure does not belong?

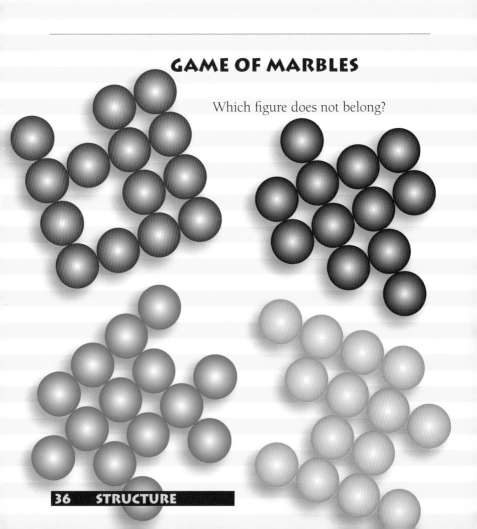

PARROTS...

The head of a parrot measures about 2⅓ inches (6 cm). His tail is as long as his head plus half the length of his body, which measures half of his total length. How tall is this parrot?

LINEA RECTA...

Number the squares on the lines with the numbers 1 through 16 in such a way that the sum of each line is 39.

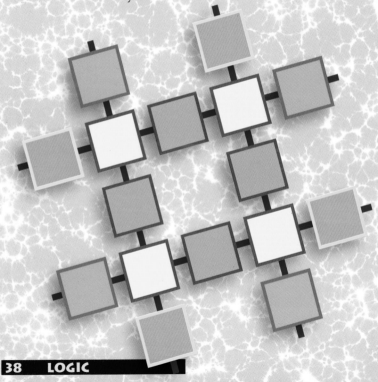

TRANSFORMATION

Can you determine what figure 4 should look like?

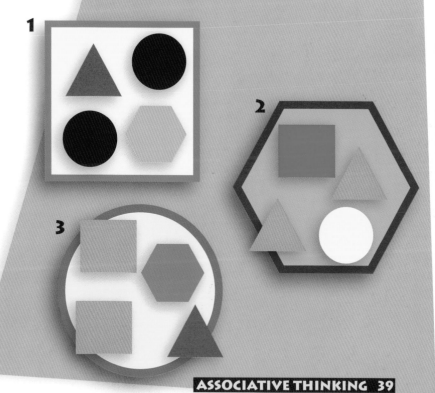

THE STABLES

Look closely at these four horses for a few moments and
try to remember their names.

Then turn to page 43 for the rest of this test.

BAROES

CHARLY

STRING

FERRON

TIP

Making a shopping list is not a sign of the softening of your brain! It's just a list of the things you need. Even so, postpone looking at it for a while after you've entered the store.

It's a good idea to organize your shopping list based on order of the aisles in the store you frequent. Read it aloud a few times before you leave the house. After a few weeks, you'll notice that you can buy about 25 of the products on the list without consulting it. By then, all you need that shopping list for is to check (before you see the cashier) whether you've forgotten anything.

DID YOU KNOW THAT...

...you become more intelligent if you go to sleep at an early hour? Studying for an exam until the middle of the night has the opposite effect. Researchers have determined that most people need six to eight hours of sleep to be able to process new information. The first and the last two hours of sleep are the most important. It is during these hours that the brain processes, organizes, and stores the new information, so that it can be put to optimal use when necessary. The advice to students is to go to sleep early the night before an exam.

P.S. Drinking cold drinks during an exam decreases brain activity.

THE STABLES

Give each horse its name back.

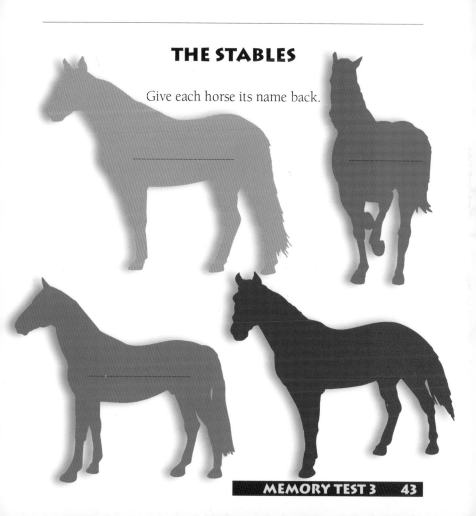

WE REGRET THAT...

This text can be found on a gravestone in Dunham, England. But somebody has made an error. Can you find it?

IN MEMORY OF

MR. EDWARD FOUNTAIN WHO
PASSED AWAY IN THIS MUNICIPALITY
ON 28 OCTOBER 1823 AT THE AGE OF
66 YEARS
AND
MRS. SARAH FOUNTAIN
HIS WIDOW WHO PASSED AWAY ON
23 SEPTEMBER 1812 AT THE AGE
OF 82 YEARS

ALL IN THE FAMILY

Each of the Bunker sons has as many brothers as he has sisters. But each of the Bunker daughters has twice as many brothers as she has sisters. How many sons and daughters are there in the family?

LINOLEUM...

How do you cut this piece of linoleum in two so that it fits exactly in a square space of 8 x 8 tiles?

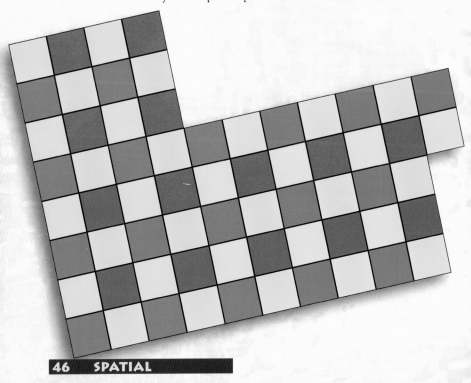

CRISSCROSS...

How many squares can you find in this crisscross?

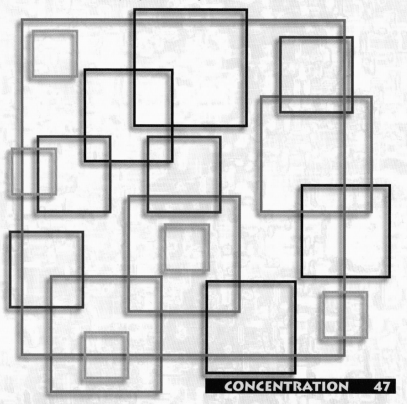

CHANGE

Cathy and Peter are on a trip to Europe. Both have the same amount of money in their pockets. How much should Peter give to Cathy if he wants her to have 1 Euro more than he?

A VARIETY OF THINGS...

Study the objects below closely for about one minute.
Then turn to page 50.

A VARIETY OF THINGS...

One object has been added and another has been changed.
Which ones?

AS QUICK AS LIGHTNING...

Is this eagle flying away from you or toward you?

HOW'S YOUR WORLD HISTORY?

Answer the following questions:

1. When did the Beatles' LP *Revolver* come out?
2. What was the intelligence agency of the USSR called?
3. Who said in 1942, "I'm going to make a car for the masses"?
4. When did the Berlin Wall come down?

SEEK AND YE SHALL FIND

Look closely at these three climbers and find the difference.

A GAME OF CHESS

Closely study the position of the pieces on the board.
Then turn to page 57 for the rest of this test.

1

2

A   **B**   **C**

TIP

Remembering telephone numbers can be a real problem. Here are a few tips to better remember a number of ten digits:

1. Divide the number into groups of 3 or 4 digits. For example, not 01 62 355 490, but 0 162 355 490.

2. Associate the groups with important dates, measurements, familiar numbers such as your age or that of people you know, your car registration number, etc.

3. Regularly write down the number.

4. Compare the groups and see if there are similarities.

5. Read the number aloud several times.

DID YOU KNOW THAT...

...many adults who had musical training before they were 12, boast a better memory for the spoken word than other people their age? When making music, your brain functions are used more actively and thus better trained. Therefore, if you start playing music at an early age, you benefit from that later in life in many other activities.

A GAME OF CHESS

Now, without looking at page 54,
return the chessmen to where
they were on the board.

ELEGANT FRENCH PUZZLE

The crosses represent three different letters, but in
such a way that the word created can be read in
28 different ways. Rack your brains, but don't break
your pencil over this puzzle!

WHAT'S NEXT?

Find the number that completes the series in a logical way.

LA CROIX BRISEE

Copy the different pieces and cut them out. Then put them on the pattern to form a cross. It looks simple, but…

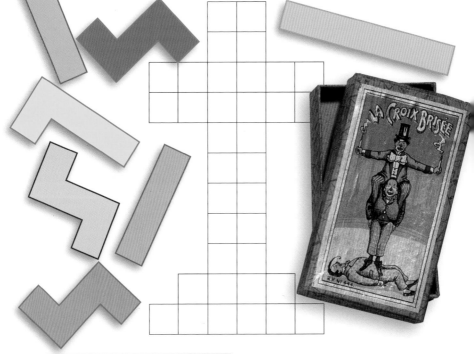

BRAVE MAYBE, BUT SMART?

These soldiers may think they're clever, but when you turn the page you'll know better…

ROPE MAKING...

A rope maker cut a rope in three pieces, which we'll call A, B, and
C to make it easy.

Rope A is 9 feet (3 m) long.

Rope B is 9 feet (3 m) plus ¼ of C.

Rope C is as long as A and B together.

How long was the rope before it was cut?

NUMBERS AND LETTERS

The letters are represented by numbers. A is only
connected with B, C, and D. C is only
connected with A and E. Where should F be?

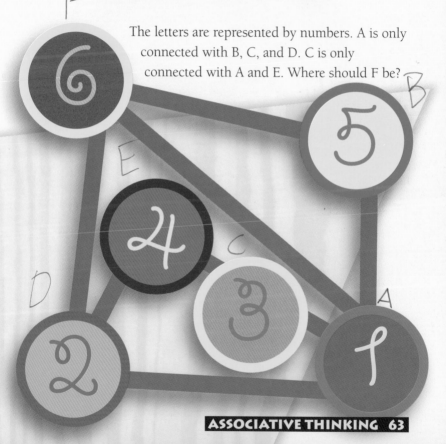

THE RIGHT SOUP-STRAINER?

Your long-term memory stores data that can be called up at certain moments. This can even happen unconsciously, in your sleep for example. When one thinks of Dalí, the famous Spanish artist, one cannot help but think of his remarkable moustache. But do you remember what it looked like exactly?
Find the right soup-strainer for Dalí.

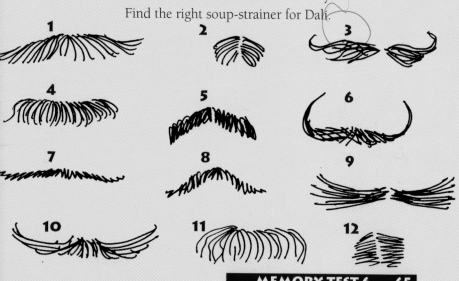

A PICKLING PROBLEM

Sprinkle some salt on a sheet of paper and some pepper over and through it. With a comb, how can you separate salt and pepper from each other again?

WITHOUT BORDERS

Which countries are being called here?

2654842
6443742
77246

TIME FOR A TEST

Look at the codes below for a minute,
then read the instructions on page 71.

12789000

21749331

00098721

TIP

Laughing is good for you! It's recommended by people who practice laughing therapy. They are convinced that laughing is good for the memory as well.

Laughing reduces stress, regulates breathing, and thus promotes mental and physical relaxation. Laughing can also function as a distraction from mental and physical suffering.

In short, all these beneficial effects no doubt benefit the memory as well.

DID YOU KNOW THAT...

... stress disturbs the memory? It has a negative effect on the attention and concentration you need when you're trying to memorize something. When we focus our attention on a disturbing element, we lose contact with the information we want to store in our memory. Stress can be even more disturbing when we try to remember something. Think of the panic of stage fright one feels before a public appearance. Actors know all too well the panic of forgetting their lines before they have to go on stage.

This fear of not remembering anything can effectively paralyze all memory circuits, albeit temporarily. Having a normal conversation will usually get these circuits functioning again and make the memory do its proper work.

TIME FOR A TEST

Try to add the right digits so the codes are complete again. Don't despair if you get only half of them right — that's actually a good score. Try to memorize the combinations of the groups of digits and where they belong.

For example, 127, 89, 000.

12**7** 9 8 00
_____

21 7 9 8 4 4 3   7 4 9 3 3 1
_____

0 0 8 9 7 2 **1**
_____

GEOMETRY BY HEART

Imagine three horizontal lines one on top of the other with 3 inches (7.5 cm) between them. Three vertical lines next to each other, also with 3 inches (7.5 cm) between them, and transecting all the horizontal lines. How many squares are created in this way?

BLACK-ON-WHITE

This puzzle is making fun of you. It is just the title of something, but how should you read it?

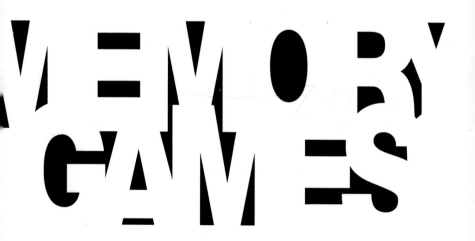

HOW'S YOUR WORLD HISTORY?

1. Where did Matthias Rust land his plane in 1987?
2. When did the first Tour de France take place?
3. What was the name of the American aid program initiated after the Second World War?
4. Which actress played the leading part in the movie *Titanic*?

IN THE FOOTSTEPS OF MONDRIAN?

Which figure does not belong here?

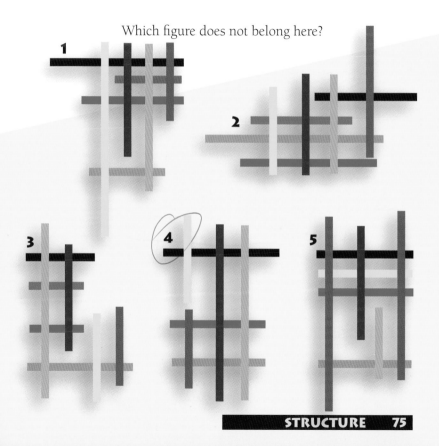

TRIGGER-HAPPY MOVIE STARS

Five famous and often trigger-happy movie stars, all a bit mixed up. That is to say, the letters of their names are a jumble. Can you order them so we know who they are?

TICNL OSTAWOED

LASECHR SORNNOB

HONJ YNEWA

RACY TRANG

UBREC SLIWIL

TARGET SHOOTING

Six shooters each shoot three times. Anthony beats Tim by two points. Tim beats Charley by two points. Charley beats Joyce by two points. Joyce beats Martin by two points and Martin beats Annie by two points. What is the score of each shooter?

6

8

15

21

36

HORSEMEN AND HORSES

Copy the illustrations and cut the three figures out. Now place the horsemen on the horses without tearing, cutting or folding the paper.

HOW'S YOUR WORLD HISTORY?

1. Where can you meet a banshee?
2. How many symphonies did Beethoven write?
3. What was Arturo Toscanini's profession?
4. What was the name of the dog guarding Hades?
5. Who painted the ceiling of the Sistine Chapel in Rome?
6. Who painted the other 15?

CALCULATING WITH DIRECTION

What is the logical next number in this series,
clockwise from top left?

FORGOTTEN FAIRY TALE

Can you find Tom Thumb?

RELATIONSHIPS

Look closely at the words below, and then turn to
page 85 for the instructions.

ORANGE - BOVEN

BLUE - KOUD

HOOFD - RED

YELLOW - GLOED

TIP

Curiosity may have killed the cat, but it's good for the memory. A curious person is interested in all sorts of things. Being curious is the best way to keep your memory active. Some people are closed off to everything except maybe one or two passions. Now it's great to be very enthusiastic about specific things of course, but for the memory it's a lot healthier to be interested in a wide variety of subjects.

DID YOU KNOW THAT...

... a distinction is made between *sensory memory, short-term memory,* and *long-term memory,* depending on how long information is stored in the memory?

Sensory memory contains the memories we associate with certain aromas, tastes, touches, images, or sounds.

Short-term memory is a practical and direct memory that is active in everything you do in your daily life. You look up a telephone number, for example, and remember it just long enough to make the call, or memorize an address just long enough to write it down.

Long-term memory is capable of containing an enormous amount of information gathered in the course of our lives. It enables us to use later in life what we have learned in our youth.

RELATIONSHIPS

Combine the words again the way they were on page 82. You should only look at that page after you've written the combinations down! Hint: Try to establish a relationship between the color and the subject to memorize it better.

BOVEN

BLUE

ORANGE

HOOFD

RED

GLOED

KOUD

YELLOW

ANAGRAMS

Presidents from then and now. The secretary who wrote their names down really had a bad day! Can you put the letters of the names in the right order again?

MYMJI RECRAT

SERYSA FARATA

SIBRO NETISLJ

OERGEG HUBS

LONSEN DELMNAA

LAB TEST

A glass container, 8 inches wide, 4 inches high, and 6 inches long, is filled halfway with mercury. Fifteen steel rods, each 1 inch wide, 1 inch thick, and 5½ inches long, are placed in it. How many of the rods are covered by the mercury?

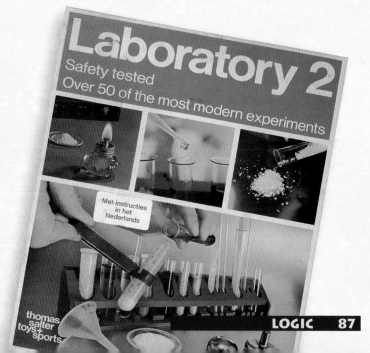

THE LONG DRIVE

A policeman lives in Texas. It takes him a few days to drive to New York City. He then returns home to Texas. All this time he is driving on the highway going south. How is this possible?

TASTY...

Put the strips with letters together to form the name of a person working in the wine business.

SUPERFLUOUS

Closely study the figure below. Four of the numbered figures on the opposite page were used to create it. Which ones?

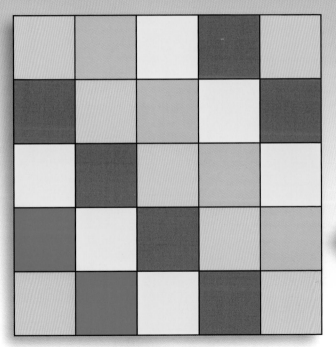

1

4

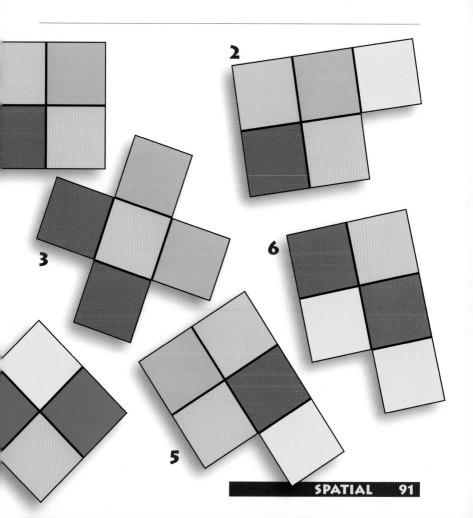

2

3

5

6

HOW'S YOUR WORLD HISTORY?

1. Who in 1927 was the first to make a solo flight from New York to Paris?
2. What is the capital of Vietnam? Seoul, Hanoi, or Saigon?
3. Guatemala's monetary unit was named after which bird: the atitlan grebe, the quetzal, or the condor?
4. Malaysia was founded in 1963. What is the name of its capital?
5. The Arc de Triomphe in Paris is located on the Place de la Concorde. Right or wrong?

CHEMISTRY?

Which numbers make the molecule at the bottom complete?

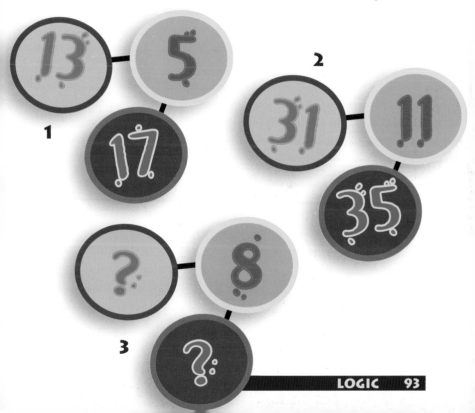

THE RIGHT LETTERS

Put a letter on every narrow line to find six words
starting with a K.

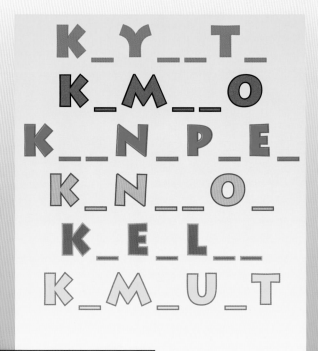

K_Y__T_

K_M__O

K__N_P_E_

K_N__O_

K_E_L__

K_M_U_T

RENOVATION

By moving just two matches the front side of the house is turned the other way.

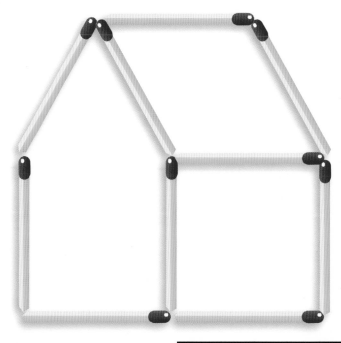

DON'T LOSE YOUR MARBLES

Look at the marbles below closely for a minute or so.
Then turn to page 99 and continue the game of marbles.

TIP

Do you find it difficult to remember TV programs or movies only a week after you've seen them? This probably has to do with the fact you see too many of them. The average adult watches TV some four hours a day. That means information pours in daily. The memory, knowing it cannot retain exact data, selects the most remarkable images and forgets the rest.

If this bothers you: watch less TV! It's probably the only solution.

DID YOU KNOW THAT...

... your life can be thrown off balance at any given moment due to far-reaching changes? Your mind then has to regain its equilibrium all over again. A new job, bereavement, birth, and divorce are some of the events that force you to take leave of the past and adapt yourself to a new situation. Aging and retirement, children moving out of the parental home, the death of parents or a partner, medical problems . . . all this can lead to a crisis which may force you to review your life.

It is this being thrown off balance that influences the functioning of the memory, not the aging process in itself.

Because your environment changes suddenly, the relationship with the outside world deteriorates and stimulation decreases.

This may lead to lack of concentration and absentmindedness, resulting in the memory being insufficiently used and stimulated.

DON'T LOSE YOUR MARBLES

A marble has been added — which one? Give the answer
before you check page 96!
Hint: There is a relationship between the numbers.
This makes remembering easier.

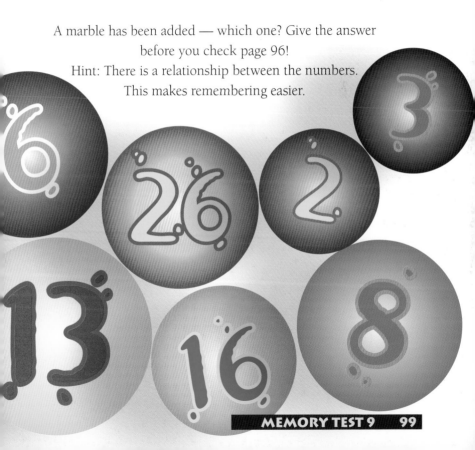

THE BLACK SHEEP

Which figure does not belong?

1

2

3

4

UNFAMILIAR AND FIERY

Do you know what this is for?

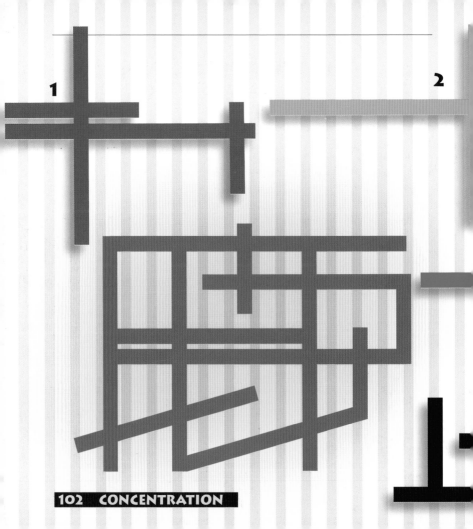

(NOT) TURNING THIS WAY AND THAT

Which of the numbered figures fit when stacked on the green one? You're not allowed to turn the figures around.

3

6

4

5

NUMBER PLATES

Which number should replace the question mark?

THE SUBTLE SQUARE

Make a cross with four matches as shown below. The puzzle is as follows: you have to create a square by moving only one match.

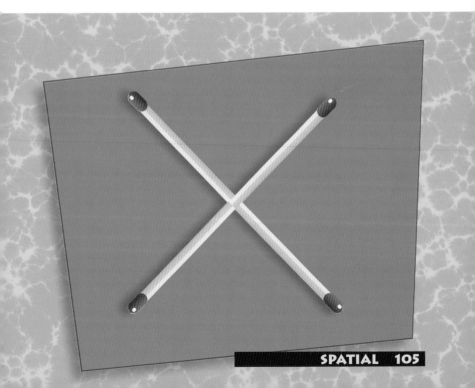

WITHOUT BORDERS

Which countries are being called here?

633375263
56732643
47435365263

HOW'S YOUR WORLD HISTORY?

1. Can you go skiing in Spain, yes or no?
2. The first public railway was constructed in Germany. Right or wrong?
3. Which African population group is called the "blue people": the Tuareg, the Dogon, or the Bedouin?
4. The first submarine was used during the American War of Independence. Right or wrong?
5. Did Vincent van Gogh leave Holland to live and work in Germany, France, or England?

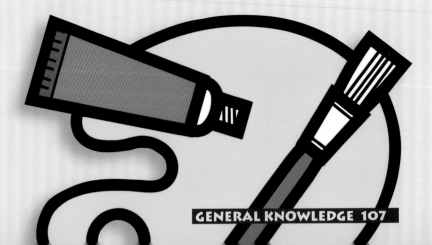

HOLE PUNCHER GONE APE

In this jumble there are three similar crosses, formed by five holes. Can you find them?

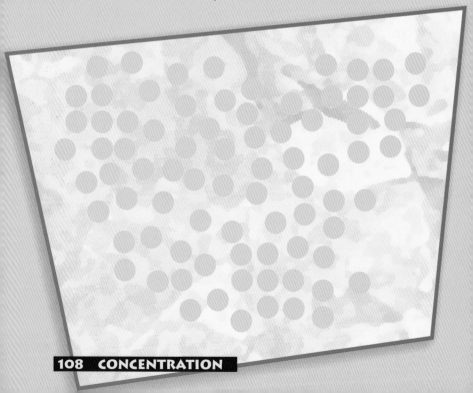

ANAGRAMS

Movie stars from the past and the present. The person who wrote out their names must have been having a mental breakdown. Can you put the letters of the names in the right order again?

INOBR MILAWILS

MOCRENA AZDI

YDOWO NLELA

RILHACE PCINLAH

KIEMYC KORURE

MOSAIC

Study this jigsaw puzzle for about a minute,
then turn to page 113.

TIP

These days there are magic memory pills on the market, available without a prescription via the Internet or in drugstores. Unfortunately memory pills do not exist. The ones advertised usually contain vitamins and a variety of plant extracts, but most of these have been proved to have no effect on the memory. It's much better to do memory exercises regularly, like crossword puzzles or repeating things aloud several times in order to remember them, or to make notes that you reread regularly. Think up memory aids.
Keeping your mind active is the best remedy.

DID YOU KNOW THAT...

... you need to live healthily for your brain and memory to function well? A balanced diet, regular sleep, and some daily exercise stimulate your brain. Certain medicines, on the other hand, and stimulants such as tobacco, alcohol, coffee, and drugs and too much stress can be fatal for the functioning of the brain.

MOSAIC

Put the figures back on their place in the plan.

DRAW THE LINE...

Connect the same letters with each other but only via the lines of the plan.
No line should cross or touch another line.

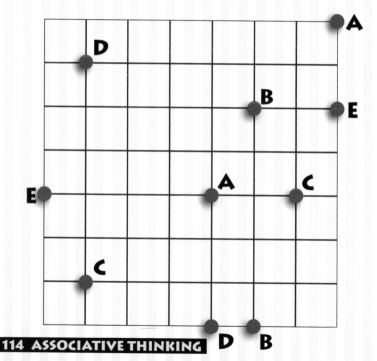

THE RIGHT LETTERS

Use every narrow line to fill in a letter and find six words beginning with an O.

O_V_O_S

O_C_P__I_N

O__E_S__E

O_L_A_T_L

O_B_D_M_N

O__R_

RUNNING

Below you see the numbers of various runners
and their running times.
Which number should replace the question mark?

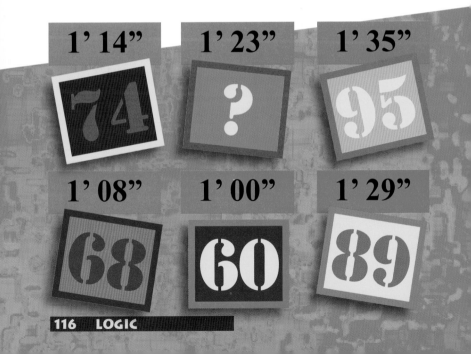

1' 14"   1' 23"   1' 35"

1' 08"   1' 00"   1' 29"

NO END...

These strips of paper represent an endless statement.

A MULTIPLE OF...

Look at the illustration on these pages below for 30 seconds and then close the book. Which figure occurs most frequently?

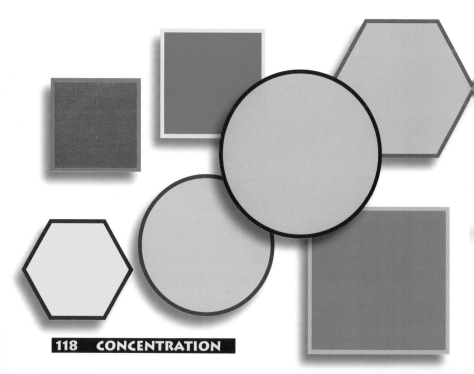

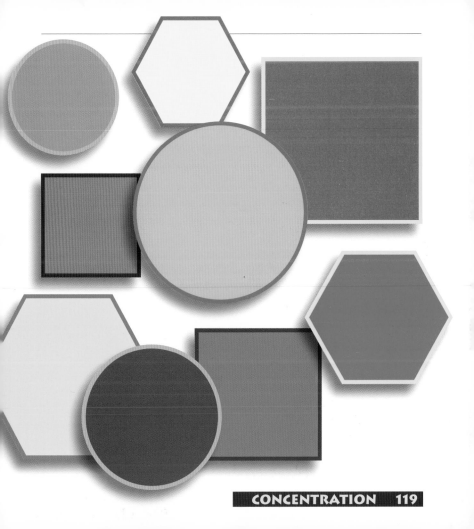

TELLING TIME...

This clock represents a mathematical sum, but the mathematical symbols (+, -, ×, and =) have disappeared. Beginning top left clockwise, can you put these symbols back where they should be so that the sum with the result 11 is correct?

TAKING THE SLOW TRAIN...

You are the engineer of a local train from White Plains, New York to New York City. And that's a distance of about 22 miles (35 km)! The train does 34 miles (55 km) per hour and makes two stops in between the two cities, one of nine minutes and one of five minutes. What is the name of the engineer?

ROCKET

THE PUZZLE OF 14 MATCHES

How do you lift 12 matches with thumb and forefinger and with the help of only two other matches?

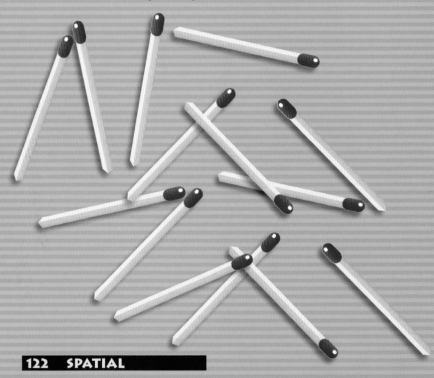

FORGOTTEN FAIRY TALE

Can you find Goldilocks?

ALPHABETICAL!

Study these three rows of letters for a minute.
Then turn to page 127

ACEGIKMOQS

BDFHJLNPRT

ADEHILMPQT

TIP

It's much more difficult to remember dates than words. The digits by themselves have no meaning. To memorize historical dates you should associate them with personal ones or link them to familiar dates or numbers such as your birth year, weight, height, and so forth.

Another method uses the so-called funnel principle. You split up the date in century, year, season, month, or day, and you link this to familiar data. July 11, 1949, for example. Last year of the first half of the twentieth century, summer, and the "crazy" number 11.

DID YOU KNOW THAT...

… by linking up diverse items, you increase the likelihood of remembering them? You do this by using the associations as a memory technique. Practicing regularly promotes the forming of linked information. The more original the associations are, the greater the chance will be that you'll remember them all. Let your imagination run wild — don't repress the images, words, and emotions that spontaneously come to mind. It'll be easier to remember things if the associative link appeals to you. This means that the connection you make between two things has significance for you or evokes a particular emotion. The shape of Italy and the leg of a soccer player, for example.

ALPHABETICAL!

Complete the lines the way they are on page 124.
Hint: Try and remember the sequence of the letters by making a
connection with their position in the alphabet.

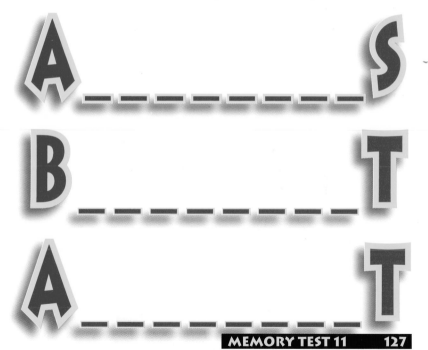

A _ _ _ _ _ _ _ _ _ S

B _ _ _ _ _ _ _ _ _ T

A _ _ _ _ _ _ _ _ _ T

THE UNKNOWN...

Thinking logically, which number should
replace the question mark?

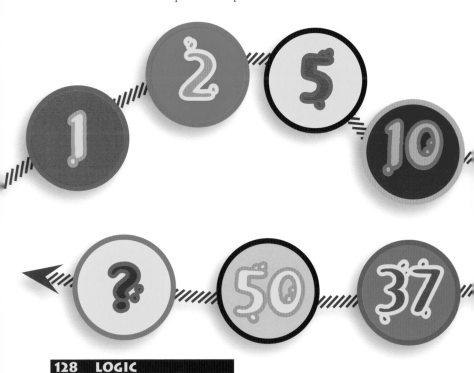

HOW'S YOUR WORLD HISTORY?

1. Canada borders which sea to the north?
2. When were the Olympic Games in Munich?
3. Who accompanied Amundsen on his first flight to the North Pole? Peary, Ellsworth, or Nobile?
4. Where is the statue of the Pissing Lad (Manneke Pis)?
5. What is the capital of Ireland?
6. The only official language of Finland is Finnish. Right or wrong?
7. Which Italian artist discovered perspective? Michelangelo, Caravaggio, or Leonardo da Vinci?

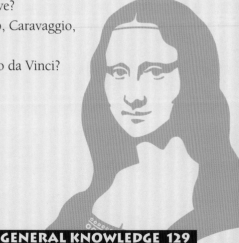

ALPHAGRAM

Which letter should replace the question mark?

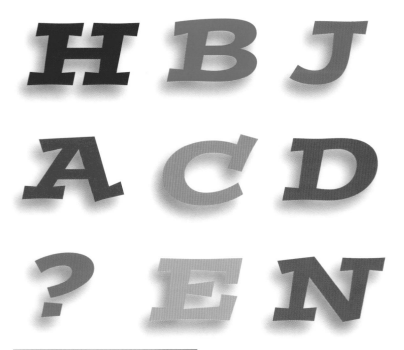

P. 8 ASIAN CONFUSION
Origami

P. 9 CONCENTRATION
No. 1

P. 10 A GAME OF CARDS
The colors (black and red) of the card symbols were swapped.

P. 16 DO YOU KNOW WHAT TIME...
Clock 4 has the right time. Clock 1 is 7 hours behind and Clock 2 (15.00) is seven hours ahead.
Clock 4 has the right time. Clock 1 (13.00) is five hours ahead and Clock 2 is five hours behind.

P. 17 ARITHMETIC
A 2. In all cases the left and the bottom numbers are multiplied and the right number added to the total, resulting in the number in the middle.

P. 18 THE RIGHT SEQUENCE?
From bottom left to top right the color of the shape in the middle becomes the color of the square next to it. The exception is the fourth from left.

P. 19 BERRY PUZZLE
Three berries. Each time a leaf is added, a berry is removed.

P. 20 A CALCULATING LOOK
Eight boards are visible.

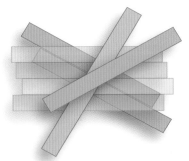

P. 21 ALPHABET PUZZLE

A	K		X	U
B	Z		M	V
C	J		N	W
D	I			Y
E	H	Q	O	T
F	G	R	P	S

P. 22–23 SEEK AND YE SHALL FIND
Second from left. Ice creem instead of ice cream.

P. 23 HOW'S YOUR WORLD HISTORY?
1. Neil Armstrong
2. Mary Quant
3. Henry Ford
4. Roald Amundsen

P. 24 A QUESTION OF COINS

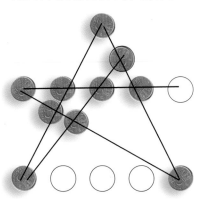

P. 25 HIDDEN NUMBER
15. There is a logical sequence, starting with 2. Clockwise: +3 (=5), -2 (=3), +5 (=8), +3 (=11), -2 (=9), +5 (=14), + 3 (=17), -2 (=15).

P. 30 AN INSEPARABLE DUO
Take hold of the string at A and pull it through the loop around the wrist of the other, over the hand and back through the loop.

P. 31 FAMOUS MOVIE STARS
Greta Garbo
Mae West
Elizabeth Taylor
Doris Day
Grace Kelly

P. 33 THE FLOATING DOT
It's exactly in the middle.

P. 34 LOOK FOR THE WOMAN OF THE HOUSE

P. 35 BRAINTEASER
A very difficult puzzle. The letters represent their position in the alphabet. Per line these positions count up to 10.

P. 36 GAME OF MARBLES
The top right figure. The others all have five rows of four marbles.

P. 37 PARROTS
The parrot is about 19 inches (48 cm) long.

P. 38 LINEA RECTA

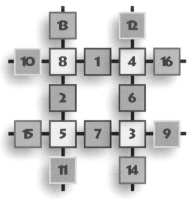

P. 39 TRANSFORMATION
Each time a square changes into a triangle, a triangle changes into a square, a circle into a triangle, and a rhomb into a circle.

P. 44 WE REGRET THAT…
If Mrs. Fountain died before her husband, how could she be his widow?

P. 45 ALL IN THE FAMILY
Four sons and three daughters.

P. 46 LINOLEUM…
See the figure at the right.

P. 47 CRISSCROSS
23 squares.

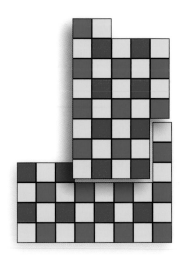

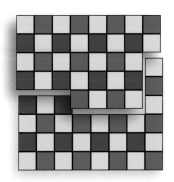

P. 48 CHANGE
Peter needs to give her only 50 cents; she then has 50 cents more and he has 50 cents less, making the difference 1 Euro.

P. 49–50 A VARIETY OF THINGS
A yellow marker has been added and the dice has been changed.

P. 51 QUICK AS LIGHTNING
It's a question of determining the direction in your mind before you look.

P. 52 HOW'S YOUR WORLD HISTORY?
1. 1966
2. KGB
3. Adolf Hitler (The Volkswagen)
4. 9 November 1989

P. 53 SEEK AND YE SHALL FIND
The second. The H is missing in the name on the cap.

P. 58 ELEGANT FRENCH PUZZLE...
MADAM. All directions according to the arrows. And then backwards as well.

P. 59 WHAT'S NEXT?
2235. Starting with 12, each number is multiplied by 2 and the new number is written backward.

P. 60 LA CROIX BRISEE

P. 62 ROPEMAKING

A is 9 feet (3 m), C has to be 9 + 9 feet (3 + 3 m) plus ¼ of itself. That's why, ¾ of C is 18 feet (6 m) which makes C 24 feet (8 m) and B 5 meters. This means the total length of the rope was 448 feet (16 m).

P. 63 NUMBERS AND LETTERS

F takes the place of the 5. 1=B, 2=A, 3=E, 4=C, 5=F, 6=B or D.

P. 65 THE RIGHT SOUP STRAINER

No. 6

P. 66 A PICKLING PROBLEM?

First you comb your hair a few times and then you hold the comb close to the salt and pepper without touching it. Thanks to static electricity, the pepper will "jump" against the comb and the salt will stay where it is.

P. 67 WITHOUT BORDERS

Bolivia
Nigeria
Spain

P. 72 GEOMETRY BY HEART

Four squares are created.

P. 73 BLACK-ON-WHITE

Memory Games

P. 74 HOW'S YOUR WORLD HISTORY?

1. Moscow's Red Square
2. 1903
3. The Marshall Plan
4. Kate Winslet

P. 75 IN THE FOOTSTEPS OF MONDRIAN?

No. 4. All the others have 4 horizontal and 4 vertical lines. This figure misses one horizontal line.

P. 76 TRIGGER-HAPPY MOVIE STARS

1. Clint Eastwood
2. Charles Bronson
3. John Wayne
4. Cary Grant
5. Bruce Willis

P. 77 TARGET SHOOTING

Each shooter's score differs a multiple of two from that of the other shooter. That's why the total score consists of the same number of uneven and even numbers.

Anthony	37 (8+8+21)
Tim	35 (6+8+21)
Charley	33 (6+6+21)
Joyce	31 (8+8+15)
Martin	29 (6+8+5)
Annie	27 (6+6+15)

P. 78 HORSEMEN AND HORSES

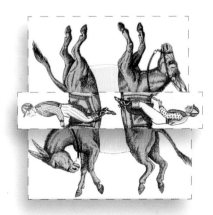

P. 79 HOW'S YOUR WORLD HISTORY?

1. In Ireland
2. Nine
3. Conductor
4. Cerberus
5. Michelangelo
6. They don't exist (joke).

P. 80 CALCULATING WITH DIRECTION

6. All the following numbers consist of the multiplication of the 2 digits of the previous number.

$4 \times 7 = 28$
$2 \times 8 = 16$
$1 \times 6 = 6$

P. 81 FOR-GOTTEN FAIRY TALE

P. 86 ANAGRAMS
Jimmy Carter
Yasser Arafat
Boris Yeltsin
George Bush
Nelson Mandela

P. 87 LAB TEST
Not even one, because steel floats on mercury.

P. 88 THE LONG DRIVE
He lives in Texas, but he started his trip to the north of New York.

P. 89 TASTY
Viticulturist

P. 90 SUPERFLUOUS
No. 1 does not belong.

P. 92 HOW'S YOUR WORLD HISTORY?
1. Charles Lindbergh
2. Hanoi
3. After the quetzal
4. Kuala Lumpur
5. Wrong (it's on the Place de l'Étoile)

P. 93 CHEMISTRY?
In each of the molecules the sum of the red and green atoms is the same as 6 times the blue ones. Moreover the red atom is as much as the green one plus 4. This means you're looking for two numbers the sum of which is equal to $6 \times 8 = 48$ and the difference 4: 26 for the red ones and 22 for the green ones.

P. 94 THE RIGHT LETTER
Keynote
Kimono
Kidnapper
Kingdom
Kremlin
Kumquat

P. 95 RENOVATION

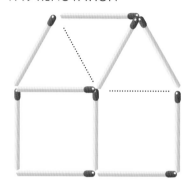

P. 100 THE BLACK SHEEP
No. 4 does not belong. No squares are formed here with the lines.

P. 101 UNFAMILIAR AND FIERY
A lighter. Scraping the rod against the flat item causes a shower of sparks.

P. 104 NUMBER PLATES...
14. Per rectangle the sum of the numbers per diagonal is the same.

P. 105 THE SUBTLE SQUARE...
There will be a very little square in the middle.

P. 106 WITHOUT BORDERS
Netherlands
Jordan
Greece

P. 107 HOW'S YOUR WORLD HISTORY?
1. Yes
2. Wrong (In Surrey, England)
3. The Tuareg
4. Right
5. In France

P. 108 HOLE PUNCHER GONE APE

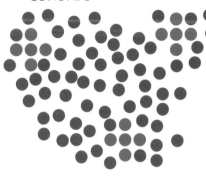

P. 109 ANAGRAMS
Robin Williams
Cameron Diaz
Woody Allen
Charlie Chaplin
Mickey Rourke

P. 114 DRAWING THE LINE...

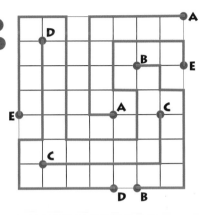

P. 115 THE RIGHT LETTER
Obvious
Occupation
Offensive
Oilcartel
Ombudsman
Opera

P. 116 RUNNING
83. The seconds of the time run added to each other make up the runner's number.

P. 117 NO END
Continuous.

P. 118 A MULTIPLE OF...
The square occurs six times, the other figures five times.

P. 120 TELLING TIME...
$12 \times 1 - 3 - 5 + 6 - 8 + 9 = 11$.

P. 121 THE SLOW TRAIN
He is called what you're called!

P. 122 THE 14 MATCHES PUZZLE

P. 123 FORGOTTEN FAIRY TALE

P. 128 THE UNKNOWN...
65. Starting with 1, the following series of numbers is created:
+1+3+5+7+9+11+13+15.

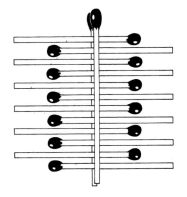

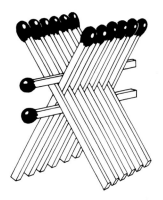

P. 129 HOW'S YOUR WORLD HISTORY?
1. The Arctic Ocean
2. In 1972
3. Elsworth
4. In Brussels
5. Dublin
6. Wrong. Swedish is an official language as well
7. Leonardo da Vinci

P. 130 ALPHAGRAM
The letter I. The letters represent their position in the alphabet (A=1, B=2, etc.). The first letter plus the second letter is the third letter, both horizontal and vertical.

Translated from the Dutch by Carla van Splunteren.

Library of Congress Cataloging-in-Publication Data Available

2 4 6 8 10 9 7 5 3 1

Published by Sterling Publishing Co., Inc.
387 Park Avenue South, New York, NY 10016

Published originally under the title *Memory Games:*
Exercises, Test, Tips and Bits of Information to Keep Your Memory Fit
© 2006 Bookman International by Bussum, the Netherlands, and Jack Botermans,
Amsterdam, the Netherlands
© 2007 by Sterling Publishing Co., Inc.

Distributed in Canada by Sterling Publishing
c/o Canadian Manda Group, 165 Dufferin Street
Toronto, Ontario, Canada M6K 3H6
Distributed in the United Kingdom by GMC Distribution Services
Castle Place, 166 High Street, Lewes, East Sussex, England BN7 1XU
Distributed in Australia by Capricorn Link (Australia) Pty. Ltd.
P.O. Box 704, Windsor, NSW 2756, Australia

Sterling ISBN-13: 978-1-4027-3651-3
ISBN-10: 1-4027-3651-7

For information about custom editions, special sales, premium and
corporate purchases, please contact Sterling Special Sales
Department at 800-805-5489 or specialsales@sterlingpub.com.